T0068990

Palm Reading in Winter

BOOKS OF POEMS BY IRA SADOFF

Settling Down (1975)
Palm Reading in Winter (1978)
Maine: Nine Poems (1981)
A Northern Calendar (1982)
Emotional Traffic (1990)
Grazing (1998)
Barter (2003)
True Faith (2012)

Palm Reading in Winter

IRA SADOFF

Carnegie Mellon University Press
Pittsburgh 2014

Library of Congress Control Number: 2014932851
ISBN: 978-0-88748-588-6
Printed and bound in the United States of America

10 9 8 7 6 5 4 3 2 1

Palm Reading in Winter was first published by Houghton
Mifflin Company, Boston, in 1978.

First Carnegie Mellon University Press Classic
Contemporaries Edition, September 2014

Acknowledgment is made to the following publications for poems or versions
of poems which appeared in them:

The American Poetry Anthology: "My Father's Leaving"; *American Review:*
"Renoir: Luncheon of the Boating Party"; *Antaeus:* "In the Future"; *Esquire:*
"Alienation from Nature"; *The Hudson Review:* "Windows," "Shelter Island,
1952," "Suite Française"; *The Iowa Review:* "The Living Room (1941–43) :
Balthus," "The Temptation to Exist: Overview, Texas"; *The Mississippi Re-
view:* "Someone Plays the Piano"; *The New Yorker:* "Goya"; *The Northwest
Review:* "Gauguin, Misunderstood, Writes a Letter to His Estranged Wife
(1890) ," "The Ancestors and What They Left," "The Marriage Bed"; *The
Ohio Review:* "The Day We Learned Manners"; *The Paris Review:* "The
Romance of the Racer," "The Romance of the Real World," "The Romance
of the Regiment," "The Romance of the Remainder," "The Romance of the
Retreat," "The Romance of the Rose"; *Poetry:* "Migration," "Meditation,"
"Palm Reading in Winter," "Reflection of a Young Woman by a Lake," "The
Transcendentalist"; *Poetry Now:* "Poem after Apollinaire," "Recollection with
Foreshadowing"; *Salmagundi:* "Pure Intelligence"; *Shenandoah:* "Landscape
with Wallace Stevens," "1917"; *Tri-Quarterly:* "The Romance of the Radish,"
"The Romance of the Restless."

Contents

I.

The Ancestors and What They Left   3
The Transcendentalist   5
1917   6
The Living Room (1941–43) : Balthus   8
The Marriage Bed   9
Goya   10
Notes from a Civil War Journal   11
Renoir: Luncheon of the Boating Party   12
Reflection of a Young Woman by a Lake   14
Gauguin, Misunderstood, Writes a Letter to His Estranged Wife
   (1890)   15

II.

Migration   19
Shelter Island, 1952   20
Recollection with Foreshadowing   21
The Execution of the Rosenbergs   22
Meditation   23
My Father's Leaving   24
Depression Beginning in 1956   25
The Day We Learned Manners   27
Alienation from Nature   28
In the Future   29
Windows   30

III.

Palm Reading in Winter   33
Landscape with a Passing Train   34
Suite Française   35
Someone Plays the Piano   36

A Clear Sky   37
Poem after Apollinaire   38
The Temptation to Exist: Overview, Texas   39
This Obsession   40
Landscape with Wallace Stevens   41
Pure Intelligence   42

IV.

The Romance of the Rose   45
The Romance of the Racer   46
The Romance of the Restless   47
The Romance of the Retreat   48
The Romance of the Radish   49
The Romance of the Regiment   50
The Romance of the Real World   51
The Romance of the Remainder   53

I.

"History cannot be more certain
than when he who creates the things
also narrates them."

— Vico, *The New Science*

The Ancestors and What They Left

On the earth's thin crust, there's a thread, a residue.
Some of the dead rising to the surface.
My great uncle and my aunt, grandfather
putting on his shoe. There's the hull
of the boat that brought him here, now a fist
of coal. Grandmother left her scent
on the doorknob, a voiceprint in the air.

What we used to call debris now helps us
breathe: this tree's leaves
contain my father's veins, its steam
a reminiscence of his breath.
This loneliness will pass, this feeling
off center. In a moment you'll leave the room
of this world and not return. What doors
have not been opened, what more could we ask for?

On my hand there's a line which extends
beyond my life, its love and fame: it's a chain
that ties me to my past.
I'm on the dock, waving
to the Jews I am, disguised as bureaucrats
with secretaries I love, officials I can't stand.

Before that, on the farm, the vodka and potatoes,
I carry their sprout and smell. And the pastoral
sense of the salt lick, the tremor, cows
kneeling on a hill. Underneath, in the damp
graveyard that extends from the earth's surface
to its core, someone's father whispering
I'm pushing through the dust that I've become

And in my head I hear his longing and his call.
We're like two figures touching

in a mirror, a trick to find out which is us.
And if I light a candle, pass my palm above the flame,
the smudge that's left — that dark streak, that film —
becomes my sign, the hillside of my own terrain.

The Transcendentalist

I remember that day in Brewster, Mass.
I was standing in a meadow, shoots of grass
bending over my shoes. Dark clouds.
A pallor on the sand dunes and gravestones.
I trembled when the rains came.
That same morning I'd been overpowered
by the August sunlight, I saw myself
in the water's reflection, a fainting child.
I have been small and thought myself smaller.
So what could I do when the ants fought
over that crumb of bread? I sat and wept.
But now I'm at home here, among friends.
I offer you the walnut shell, its mindless
protection. Its seeds, the germination of evening.
Let's not speak of death. I say this:
I was formed by the earth, and am.
I do not chastise its mystery, our slight
discrepancy. I welcome its pull, its release.
I love the world, but would not choose to live there.

1917

That evening we turned to another country.

We found our refuge in the river.
We began rowing against the tide
of events, our thoughts carried us
to another age and place. You asked,
"What will happen to the trees
of the enemy, the ancient palace

we adored? If we're no longer children
of the czar, what place have we on the shore
of someone else's land? Do you remember when we
were poor, when all the bright stars were out
of reach? Weren't we hungry then for an event
which would change our course, or the coarseness

of others we abhorred? If we are reactionary now,
what do we react against? The bad manners
of the poor, the overcoats of muslin and gauze,
anything that makes us mourn more for others
than ourselves. Now we are here, and our boat drifts
far away from shore. Shhh. I think I hear

fish floating to the surface, curious
about our deaths and theirs, all of us
strangers to sunlight and air. Sister,
what is it you hear?" I rowed without speaking,
I thought of the oar's tongue in the water's
mouth, a candle's dripping lips. I knew

we could not live without borders, with nothing
between us and the water's edge. Then, at sunrise,
we saw the city's ashes, the smoke that slowly

cleared. I tried my best to row and steer
while you rolled into a ball of sleep
on the boat's wooden floor, rocking back

to a childhood we found no need to live.

The Living Room (1941–43): Balthus

Music meant everything to the father, but his two daughters are sleepy now: one has dozed off on the couch and left the living room a mess: the brown felt tablecloth covers half the cocktail table and the bowl of fruit could tumble at any moment. The younger daughter is doing her best to study composition, but her eyes too are wandering inward; her daydreams are still simple, she thinks of ordinary things: of skipping rope in a schoolyard, teasing a girl friend about the length of a dress, the discipline of kneeling in a shelter while bombers fly overhead.

Mother is still working in the factory, well past dinnertime, and father will be home late, if at all. The piano, which was intended for their lessons and bought at a considerable expense, stands idle in the corner, hardly visible. After the first child was born mother promised father the melodies of Mozart would sweep through the house; now anything vaguely German must be whispered secretly, and the music played is mostly French, some faint impression.

Earlier today there was a hint this household was not so intact. The older sister held the younger in her arms when she was frightened by a noise, there was the slightest hint of a caress, the reflection of a hand against a thigh. So much tenderness comes forth of fear these days, this should not cause surprise. And when the parents arrive to collapse on that same couch, no words of passion will be expressed. The adults save their purest feelings for the enemy, and all they share is sleeping now, where everything is permitted, and nothing is quite done.

The Marriage Bed

Tonight the Russian roofs are blue
in the evening light. The neighbors' windows
dark on both sides — no candles,
no one reading by firelight.
They're all asleep but us, rising
and falling on the marriage bed.
Who's afraid of the Poles tonight, or the soldier
drunk, in search of who knows what?
Remember this afternoon, when we huddled
against a storefront in the crowd?
Or how the chicken pecked,
senseless, on the cobblestones? That's
how I feel kissing you on the cheek,
when we're lost on our own straw bed.
It was the glare of others that frightened us
then: a match lit up against a bench, a stranger
rubbing against your breast. Something bright
shining in the sunlight: a weapon, a flash of steel.
Now it's dark enough for everyone. And so quiet
sleepwalkers could walk the streets.
But why think of them? We're safe enough,
and I could sleep tonight if I had reason to.

Goya

It is night so you can shoot me.
I'm no rich man, what difference could it make?
Yet there are certain things I'm aware of:
the grief of my friends, my enemies'
indifference, the king's palace, its dull
shine against this cloudless night.
And the blood of my father by my side.
The crops and the cicadas go on perfectly well
without me: I am of no importance, a man
with a family, enough children to make me weep.
Go ahead and shoot. Relieve me of my misery.
I'd kill you if I had the chance.
All I ask for is a little music, a small
ceremony for my death: the orchestration
of the king's militia, the silver instruments,
the guns' voices before the chorus of wounds.

Notes from a Civil War Journal

after Matthew Brady

We bathe in a tin tub
heated by a stove.
The pure ache of the physical —
muscle against bone. Today
was ordinary: we struck branches
with an ax, cooked sausage over wood.
I milked a goat and thought of cheese.
Trees fall in our path; we cross
the same small stream again and again.

The war is almost over, someone said.
But I'm filled with doubts
and I'm afraid. I miss my wife,
though I can't remember what she's like.

Yesterday a town was burned, children
wept into the ash. I discovered Georgia
was real, not just a sound on our lips.
I'm learning things I don't want to know.
Oh Lord, help us not to want too much.
I can survive the body's suffering
and the wounds. But the mind's wandering
is endless, without release. Change
me into something simple, something
to be used. For the weather's cold and life
in the ditches does not go far enough.
We're soldiers, our hands get cold,
and we need to be held, like anyone.

Renoir: Luncheon of the Boating Party

for Richard Howard

I'm the only one here who wants to have a serious talk; Uncle Max seems willing to listen, but he can hardly keep his eyes open. "What do you know of the Blacks?" he says. "Were it not for our adventures in Africa, your father wouldn't have a sailboat to sail on the Loire." So what, I think to myself, what's so wonderful about the Loire, with all its ugly driftwood piled up on shore? Who wants to be here or there? There's so much food I'm almost sick to my stomach; all those vulgar colors, the orange canopy, the green grapes, that heavy purple wine, are all part of a conspiracy to make me dizzy; that's why I prefer to remain in the background.

Of course I could not converse with the women the way *they* do. Like Édouard and his contemptible good manners: he knows how to hold a glass of wine, how to put his arm around a girl. After all, he's been away. And it's so sickening how the women pretend to be interested in the men, in all their meaningless chatter. Who cares if the sun has never shone this brightly, about the advances in photography, the latest farce about declining manners in the provinces? And that coquette Marie, pretending to cover her ears while Georges brags about his latest conquest, the maid who makes dresses for the new boutique. Only Félice seems above it all; she'd rather talk to her dog than the animals at this table. She's the one I dream about when I'm alone in bed.

I keep thinking, how do I look when I smoke a pipe? Do I look ridiculous, do I look too young? I hate to be ridiculed, especially by the women slightly older, the ones who think they know everything about the world and more. What I say to them goes unheard or seems unheard of. All because my hair is red and my beard is not quite filled in. If only I did not blush so easily. I wonder, if I lost myself in the marshes, would anyone seek me out? Would anyone miss me in the slightest?

I have a silly daydream, of all of us floating out to sea on a dinner plate. Everyone else is so busy talking, trying to draw attention to himself, that I'm the only one who notices. How long would it take for them to get the picture? What if we were lost at sea, what would all these bright colors mean? Who would care about a shade of lipstick, the rouge on a woman's weeping cheek? How long would it take for us to recall the meaning of hunger, what would we talk about? The declining bodies of one another, the disappearance of the land, the rain we'd have to face part of every single day?

Reflection of a Young Woman by a Lake

Disease was spreading on the lawn.
In the house she occupied
she was growing up to find the snails
and slugs sucking on the leaves; important
to their survival was the death of what
they loved.
       And how, in the morning's chill,
it reminded her of a man she saw once
floating in the lake, not dead but passive
in his acceptance of where the water took him.
She watched him for hours, not desiring
him but what he desired, that restfulness
in motion, the ability to take in
whatever sun there was.
       Then he passed
from her sight, she was left with an image
of hopelessness — how she'd have to move
from what she loved, continuously, in and out
of sight of others who passed their time
with her, or gave the passing chance to leave
this world she lingered in: that luxury
of leisure which made thoughts of future loss
so wrong to think about, so hard to ignore.

Gauguin, Misunderstood, Writes
a Letter to His Estranged Wife (1890)

Things were not so simple there,
though the air was thin and mildly
sexual, the moist wind moved its way
through my straw hat. The iguana's tongue
would lash at my tanned legs. For breakfast
I ate mangoes, and hollowed out
coconuts for all my toasts. If I were
not quite native in my stance, the foreign
soon enough became familiar, the brown
skinned women's breasts did not excite me
so much as yours. In truth, I must confess
I did not waste my time, if I kept it at all.

When I came back, the customs
office asked what I wanted to declare,
and I could think of nothing but myself.
But then I saw you again, your hair
still caught in a net, the bonnet you wore
made with someone else's industry. That night
in bed I felt little had been lost
on the mainland, and the language we spoke
could be deciphered in the sand I walked on,
or the busy street where you held a stranger's hand.

II.

"Let the world carry me away
and I will have memories."

— PAUL ELUARD, *"Inside the Cylinder of Tribulations"*

Migration

This is our last day together,
the day the birds fly south.
The groundhog burrows in
for winter. The sun shines less.
There is a relation between us
and the events we endure:
when there is motion
in the trees, a rustling not unlike
the removal of your dress, something moves
in me. And I know this distance
between us exists somewhere else.
In the season's change, the swoon
of a leaf, the melodrama of a threatened
snow. Now I am here. You are moving
away from my bed. If the birds
are not sad, their singing seems so
to me; their flight, like the moment
of your leaving, disturbs the air
I breathe, seems inevitable and trite,
but moves me now nonetheless.

Shelter Island, 1952

A space opens in the trees,
there's a child in the clearing.
Suits with padded shoulders, "Memories of You"
twisting on the phonograph. A simple house
with shutters, shaded from the weather, but it's a storm
you remember. The sky crowding in
with gray, a wind so warm it curls
the leaves. Father's out tonight,
you're unsure when he'll return. Mother's
in her slip, sleeping by the fan.

You're supposed to be sleeping too,
in the cellar where it's cool. Instead
you're reading magazines on the bed.
Who knows what you're afraid of?

The screen door opens
and lets no one in. On the roof, branches
are tapping, that's all. The threat
of rain passes, it doesn't justify your fear.
And late tonight, when you're asleep,
father will return, though he'll leave again.
You walk outside, there's no one there
to speak or draw you close. Then what was it
the wind left as a gift? The arms
of trees arching toward the ground,
a boy surrounded by the past's debris,
the petals of flowers discarded in their beds.

Recollection with Foreshadowing

You do not remember this: the ice storm which swept the city soon after you were born. Your father carries a bottle of milk in his hand, your mother's scarf covers her face. The ice is thick and glossy as a young woman's thigh; you could not see yourself in it, nor would you dare to try. This is the fifth year of your parents' marriage, so there is another woman in the background, though she is facing some other direction, waving her hand, perhaps calling a cab. Your mother would rather not notice the distracted look on your father's face, so she does not. Instead she thinks of you in their warm house, the risk she is taking to bring you fresh milk. If only you had a fireplace, she thinks; soon you will move to a larger house, one where you'll have your own room and at last sufficient heat. When they get home and close the door behind them, the world seems suddenly warmer, your father rubs his cold hand against your mother's cheek. And yet the sound of his palm against her face is like a match about to ignite — something is burning in the air, something angry is about to be said. But the sound of your young voice is for the moment comforting, and when your mother lifts you out of the crib she whispers with her cold breath words not meant for your ears, but with a message you will not soon enough forget.

The Execution of the Rosenbergs

That summer father moved farther away,
framed by a larger event: a President
elected, the Communists uncovered
and two Jews executed in their place.
So mother mourned a parallel of deaths,
losses to be measured against the past.

At the march I was confused by the masses
of people gathered, a stranger's breath
and tears. Could they have known
what my father meant? It seems a long time ago,
the personal life, the tiny room
I lived in as a child. But there is a photograph

which opens up almost like a porch
looking out to a field: a family's
out there, sitting on the weeds
calling flowers by improper names.
Then someone's called away, then another,
till the field is the future's

reflecting glass. Someone's called to the gallows,
grandfather spits on the czar
when he's asked to serve, father drives off
in his Chevrolet. The road's terminal,
he can't turn back. The lights dim
momentarily, then the Jews

who inhabited this earth illuminate
the flesh, then flake to ash.
Who's to blame? The slogans at the march
don't seem strong enough, but the Communists
are partly right: everything's a struggle,
and to forget the past is to give up hope.

Meditation

"Is anything central?" — John Ashbery

One event stands out from childhood:
the day someone left.
The house was not empty,
but it would happen again
and again. This affected my sight:
fragments filled the air
with everything — a man
standing by a door, an owl
in daylight, evenings by myself.

Certain contradictions recurred:
a streetlamp glowing at sunrise,
the moon rising in the afternoon.
Now a white sheet covers everything,
a network of cloth, a web on the door.

Perhaps this explains nothing
but a restlessness to leave the world,
the desire to sleep on the floor
of one's past, beyond the rise of memory.
Once, someone left. The world was not changed
as I was, but the house I lived in
was left by itself, a thin frame standing
against the past and parting of events.

My Father's Leaving

When I came back, he was gone.
My mother was in the bathroom
crying, my sister in her crib
restless but asleep. The sun
was shining in the bay window,
the grass had just been cut.
No one mentioned the other woman,
nights he spent in that stranger's house.

I sat at my desk and wrote him a note.
When my mother saw his name on the sheet
of paper, she asked me to leave the house.
When she spoke, her voice was like a whisper
to someone else, her hand a weight
on my arm I could not feel.

In the evening, though, I opened the door
and saw a thousand houses just like ours.
I thought I was the one who was leaving,
and behind me I heard my mother's voice
asking me to stay. But I was thirteen
and wishing I were a man I listened
to no one, and no words from a woman
I loved were strong enough to make me stop.

Depression Beginning in 1956

for Jon and Barbara

This mood's not mirrored in the weather, raining,
nor can it be cured
by the usual remedies. It is a mood, unlike the geography
of rivers, without a source, all too general,
like a conversation with a stranger, a way of living
you've adjusted to. Only you haven't
shaken the feeling something's wrong, your wife is off
with someone else, or you would like to be.

Your father sitting in a chair one July is a thought
you have now, in a time before air conditioners, sweating
through his shirt. You think you know what he is thinking:
should he buy a new house, get a divorce,
should he vote for a Democrat who has no chance to win,
should he help your mother in the kitchen though he doesn't
want to see her again? He's not sitting in that chair now
so he must have moved. Or something moved in him. The lesson
you want to learn is how we change ourselves,
how we move from past to future.

                                   If we follow
the movement of flowers and trees, which we don't, we would know
it's not through consciousness — the lilac
that blooms at night knows nothing of that change.
Nor is it something large, what we do in the eyes
of others — what do the branches care for the leaves
when they grow up or down?

                                   And yet your father
is remarried, he voted for a Democrat, he's somewhere
else in Arizona, free of trees, at last something good
is happening to him. Why couldn't it be your mood
that's changed, what would it take to remove yourself

from this feeling, this weight of the present
mood of helplessness? It is not a great disaster
that makes us change, but a straightening
of will combined with circumstance: nature
has nothing to do with it now, though it might
have in the past, when we understood the motion
of animals against the trees.

                  For we are not animals
now, nor could we choose to be: though we choose sometimes
the pastoral and lovely, it is never quite enough
to leave the melancholy we've come to know,
and if that mood should pass we think it was
some miracle or strength or someone else we love
coming to our aid. And we'd be wrong in part and right
in ways we can't define in love or sometimes change.

The Day We Learned Manners

There was a garden and a lake.
We learned how to say thank you, women
before men, how not to talk
with our mouths full. Our parents
were full of small talk, while we watched
the boats move in and out of our sight.
The trees were rigid and the air
was chilled. When we went swimming, you confessed
your fear of water, you moved toward me
without help. Yet it wasn't your manners
I noticed — it was the distance between us
and our parents, your breasts beginning
to bob in your sweater, the sleeves
rolled up from the wrist. In that photograph
taken later, we were two heads
without bodies, the body of water
burying the drift of what would pass between us,
the nuance of shoulders, what we would touch
and what we would not.

Alienation from Nature

We walk outside and everything
is changed: the evening dissolves
into daylight, the sun's dull balm
glosses over the larkspurs and pine.

The illness of argument
is over: your body becomes a foreign
country, my tongue's language is useless
against your lips. When the fog

burns itself off the trees, the landscape
is clear at last: now we can see
the brutality of wheat, the cutting edge
of grass, the countryside's vague desire

to disappear in the weeds.
And when I cross a small stream, the water
divides us — we feel the weight
of our bodies begin to sink, the weather's

threatening cure and the disruption of air
when we walk, gesture, or want to speak.

In the Future

Everything was what I asked for
strangers who approached me now knew my name,
my pockets were full of money, I loved my wife
and someone else.
                    Yet the world outside was not
my own: I learned to fear the ordinary, the sudden
ring of the telephone, the saucer without a cup,
the full and empty room.
                    Mornings I paced
and could not spend my time, I woke
long before the sun's dull rise. I spoke to friends
as though I were someone else, the man they expected.

The rain became my mood, its slick tongue my own
transparency, my own smooth tongue. In my bedroom
I did not recognize myself, I could not remove my clothes.
And when my wife left me, I remembered only her
empty space, that nakedness which left my own.
                    Her face appeared
out of reach in someone's car, in darkened theaters,
then not at all. Gradually it was this distance
from myself and others which saved my life:
if no one loved me now I was free to be myself.

Everything was again what I asked for: loneliness
only I could contain, the house's small rooms
my covering, my lovely suffocation. And the words
I spoke were pure as ice, the hand I offered
myself was mine — though it did not extend far
and was not unique, those I loved would recognize
its grasp, its tenderness and fear, its strength
my loss and everything I longed for.

Windows

The window's sight is small:
a branch with leaves, some trees
swaying in the background, a dimensionless
sky behind it, wavering with clouds.
Inside there is less, the home. Its desk,
shapes of furniture, so much idle thought.
The window is a bridge of glass, a surface
to see through, a stranger's face. In its frame
there is an artless picture, a dull form
in slow motion, the psychology of discontent.
There is a window in the hand's palm,
in the drinking glass. Soon enough,
it all adds up. There is a place
where the inner and outer worlds must touch,
but don't. Where yes and no make no sense.
Perhaps the vandal who breaks a window,
the burglar who travels through it, do battle
with boredom, break the surface of the world
as it appears to us. Or at night, when no world
appears beyond the window and we settle for less,
what we see in its reflection is what we want,
but don't believe in, things we couldn't bear to love.

III.

"Enough! or Too Much."
— WILLIAM BLAKE, *"The Marriage of Heaven and Hell"*

Palm Reading in Winter

Something simple, something clear.
Anticipation of cold weather, skaters
circling on a pond. The snow is void
of distance: what seems far away is all
too close. A man comes home to his family,
tired of his work. If there's a fire
in the fireplace, so much the better.
A hot drink with its steam for his lips.
So what if it's not enough?

        Think of the absence
of thought: snowdrifts over footprints,
a candle lit in sunlight. What's difficult,
retrace: the ice ballet, the figure eight.
Hands over the fire, the smell of cinders
on our clothes. The lines in the hand
are complex but change, smooth themselves out.
And if in our palms we see change that seems
unjust, the hand of someone else in ours
may mask that fear, distract us for a time
at least. What is not enough? What we have and what
we want, the need to know the ache that complicates.

Landscape with a Passing Train

Thunderclouds all day. The gray sky
dips down and narrows in, softening the hills
as we approach. This mood will change, this chill
in summer, this sadness without cause.

A train passes in the distance, its passengers
asleep: I love how they escape from place
to place. The eyelids close and the mind
drifts somewhere else. You were thoughtful as a child,

weren't you? There were meadows to walk through,
the thick grass and thistles by the swamp
where you hid. Even then you wanted the train
to stop, to see the faces still and wide awake,

for the moment not to stir, as when a deer
freezes in a clearing. Interiors would suit you best.
A still life with flowers, perhaps, the light
drifting through the domestic scene — flowers

picked so long ago the petals fade and drop.
What was the occasion for this scenery? The specific
fails, as it always must, to build a mood
removed from our histories, personal and small.

Yet this is all we have, the insufficient color
of the afternoon, the noise of the train whistling
now so far away, the sense of what's important
having quickly passed. In the hollow where we seek shade

beneath a tree, the present seems a resting place
and not the blur it is. Though we'll move on
it's the walk we'll remember, the dulling
of the leaves, and not the mood that brought us here,

the space hollowed out between the trees,
not the storm, its cause, nor the trees themselves.

Suite Française

after Poulenc

Let's recall the saxophone, the ritual
violence of the dance floor,
the tables that rose and fell
around us, the center of attention
we'd become. The tango and the waltz,
hair slicked down, water of gardenia,
water of rose. Boys in the aisles
with knives in their cumberbunds, Gauloises
sleeping on their lips and the gaze
that turned the dance floor to glue.

Wasn't it too much to bear, a longing
for the young, the partners we wanted
to exchange? Outside, on the frigid stairs,
snow on the forsythia and sycamore,
steam from your face dissolved the air.
And on the balcony of no moon, of no stars
and clouds that brought white flakes
to burn your cheek, in the thick harangue
of changing light from the chandeliers,
I thought of you as someone else
longing and dangerous to be kissed.

Someone Plays the Piano

Someone plays the piano
and the world sinks into mud.

But we're not in the world, we're somewhere
above it all: water rising to the clouds.

In the background, a man's chained
to a tree, a battle is going on.

A young couple walks through the woods.
Tender words will be said. It will snow,

then the sun will come out. Deeper and deeper
they go, they become one with the trees. We're not

moved by their words, but we'll feel the pain
of the voice, the vibrations in the chest.

A nurse pushing down on the ribs
of the sick, a form of tenderness.

A day room, a curtain which lets in light.
But we're not in the room, we're outside

looking in. Then the suspension of breath.
Human traffic comes to a halt. Someone

breaks a vase, the man who cuts meat
for a living, who has blisters on his hands.

The music stops, dark clouds pass, we return
to earth, and what remains is all that lasts.

A Clear Sky

A clear sky threatens this morning
to overtake our thoughtfulness,
forecast by no one and taking most
by surprise. Yet a few of us
will still be children standing over water
disinterested in reflection, willing
to be quieted by the shock of clouds
passing over the schoolyard so suddenly.

If all of us could leave the countryside
or at least forget the thick textures
of shadows which tend to separate, if we
could be absent as we are permanent, then endings,

which clear up so little anyway, might
make their point. But the sunshine in the yard
and the diminished wind will offer hope
we don't deserve: that frozen light
cast over children and their satchels.

Poem after Apollinaire

I miss the peace and quiet of Chicago
that's the kind of guy I am
I've been to funerals where cigars
are the only monuments to the dead and lipstick
bleeds on the dead man's lips
I'm not afraid of death and I'm not afraid
of noise but when you take off your stockings
I hear moles tearing at the seams of the earth
field mice scurry into the deepest holes
and a roar from the subway that could make me say
Yes Sir to the President who I hate

And if afterwards I should light a cigar
it has nothing to do with the movies
or having a good time it's just my way
of keeping my fingers busy
of burning your smell out of the room
I don't want to work I don't even want to smoke
I just need a few moments to recover

The Temptation to Exist: Overview, Texas

On a plain in Texas, a landscape barren as morality, a drop of water forms on the cactus leaf. A snake uncoils itself, its many spools of skin. On the rare occasion when a person enters this world, he is dressed in nineteenth-century regalia, lost in this century as the rest of us. And when a car drives past on a dirt road, it kicks up dust, clouds and clouds of dust.

Just before evening, grandmothers begin to appear on the porches. There is tobacco in the air, the vague rumblings of someone's voice. Soon something small and human will occur in the house — mother will drop a dish on the way to the kitchen table, father will push his boot through the door when his daughter disobeys him. Somewhere behind the house a teenage boy sits with his girl friend on a fence. They invent something to talk about: the virtues of evening, the cactus leaf's odd shape. "I wish I remembered the dust bowl," the girl says, "with all its swirls and swirls." When she lifts the hem of her dress to examine the floral print, the boy wants to say, "How lovely women are," but listens to the radio instead, with its three ugly tunes.

What does he care about the irony of human life, that literary invention? Tonight the world outside seems small: the stars are shriveled seeds, the hum of the locusts and june bugs so familiar they cannot be heard. When he lights a cigarette and the girl sighs, a few cinders from his hand move toward the sky — and in that light, in the bright hiss of a match, they appear both vulnerable and stark against the dull gloss of the bearable Texas heat.

This Obsession

This obsession with fame
as religion, whose star will rise
and whose will fall, who'll be saved
after death and who we'll throw away . . .
I say let the lilies fight it out
with the gazelle for the tall grass,
the lion would trample them both.

This invisible rose in the starlight,
what a thing to think of before dinner!
Why not eat a hearty meal, and then disappear?

How much better to be ignored!
Could the savior walk the streets
without being stoned, without teen-agers
tugging at his pants? If they think you're no one,
maybe you are, maybe you're the one star
who refuses to shine, the weed in the garden
that flowers at night, in the privacy
of a plateau all your own.

As for the cloud cover tonight, it's a veil
over everything: the woman you'll kiss
will be mysterious and strange, and if
she knows your name everything will be ruined
and just like her husband, ordinary as daylight,
the star that rises quickly and falls too soon.

Landscape with Wallace Stevens

I stood by the door of a grand hotel.
There was no threat of rain, the sun did not
come out. I felt the weather's absence

reflect on my white coat. If I lit
a cigar the world was suddenly brighter,
if I combed my hair the sparks flew

out and out. You descended from some floor
above me, but your mind was somewhere else:
in a cavern in Kentucky, where you'd confused

stalactites with their -mites. Or on the man
who slipped into your room, he reminded you
of someone else. If you don't know what is hanging

in the air and what holds up doubt, your glance
instructs me nonetheless. It says: you are you
and I am not. If I walked into your room

with a vase of yellow flowers, bringing light
to your pale and absent face, your lover would
not be startled, and though you might regard

my presence, you could not accept the change.

Pure Intelligence

The heat wave must be coming closer.
Your son said, "The soup has a fever."
Is that wrong? A translation from the French
perhaps? The music in the background suggests
a tempest, but was this the instrument
of its arrival, was his small claim worth the storm?

Meanwhile, the disconnection of the hours
continues: you keep floating into sleeplessness,
you ask your wife, is it day or is it night?

And the question still remains: what is pure
intelligence? An unlimited vocabulary, a concern
without a context, sunlight filtered through a fan?

The weather does seem pure but unrelated
to this mood, this foreboding from your son.
His idea made no concession to its audience,
the small steps of time or common sense. It resembled
an obsessive nightmare, a light that burned itself out.

Something indeed is burning up, being consumed
by itself. You think, it's all right, it's raining
somewhere else. But where?
                              In the next room, perhaps,
a maniac is stabbing at the heat, he can't take it,
whatever it is, this vapor of language, this wish
for continuance, the heat that could span the hours,
the mind's shape making itself clear at last.

IV.

The Romance of the Rose
and Other Tales

The Romance of the Rose

I could not help myself, I fell in love with the florist. Each day he handed me arrangements of flowers: lilies-of-the-valley, chrysanthemums and roses, exotic willows and violets. As a lover he was strange and melancholy: he had an intense hatred for the out-of-doors and almost never left the house; the mention of sports made him dizzy and a car moving too fast would bring him close to tears. When he found me talking to another man he brought me a wreath of flowers and said he would leave me, though he did not. In the winter, though, it was I who could not leave my bed: my robe seemed to grow roots on the sheets and I made him bring me my meals on a tray. When he threatened to leave I became the carnation in his lapel, I was his brooch. When the weather became warm and clear, somehow it was he who wrapped me in a blanket, dragged me outside to a park; and when we made love I was the one who wilted, I felt my color brush off on his chin. And when he took me home for the last time, I could not help but stare at the limp stems of flowers, the discolored water, the fragrance of my own immobility, the fear that all this could happen again, and when it did, nothing would blossom, nothing would spoil.

The Romance of the Racer

The race car driver was different. He made love with all his clothes on. Always the smell of grease, a trailing vapor of gasoline. He drove circles around me and when it was over I was tired and dizzy, his tongue in my mouth was a memory, a thin slice of dirt road. When he spoke he was like an engine idling, he could never talk fast enough; but whatever he said was unexpected. "I enjoy being sad," he once told me. "I wish there were more sadness in the world." In bed he was not much of a man: once was always enough.

He was an insomniac who read long books and never said a word about them. He took me to the opera and asked me not . to raise my voice. He hummed arias he said had not been written yet. Once he took me to a party where all his former lovers were, and they never stopped talking about him. Two of them he still made love to on big occasions: the night before a race, the afternoon of Verdi's birthday. And when he took me home he was unusually cautious, driving way below the speed limit, stopping at intersections where he had the right of way. When he got into bed he curled up like a wheel; in the dark I could have sworn he was spinning. In the end, what he had to prove he could not, and we all loved him the more for it, at least for a little while. When I drove out of his driveway for the last time I did not look back; but on the road I had the feeling I was constantly being passed, no matter how fast I went, no matter how many cars were filled with whistling men.

The Romance of the Restless

"Power that is not used is power abused." — Egil Krogh

If you think only men are studs, you're sadly mistaken. I've walked into bars, ordered myself a drink, harassed the man next to me, the short one with the glasses; I've rubbed my hand against his thigh. At first he was frightened and tried to pull away; he said he was married, he was waiting for someone who was on her way. I told him I'd slept with men lots uglier than he was, that's how much I'd been around. If he were married, so much the better: fewer complications. Then, after I put my arm around him, made small circles in his ear with my tongue, got him all hot and bothered, I excused myself to go to the ladies' room and sneaked out the back door, never to come back.

At parties I can be very aggressive: I walk up to the handsomest man and strike up a conversation. If he wants to talk deep, the way most men think they do, I can talk deep. I can mention Kierkegaard, de Mandiargues, Wilhelm Reich, or Otto Rank. I can tell him my psychological problems, just to let him know I can be vulnerable. I tell him, "I'm just waiting for the man who can make me enjoy it." If he wants small talk, that's also in my repertoire; I can tell when he's getting bored and that's when I rub my breast against his shoulder.

I can be cruel and I can be kind: whichever serves my purpose. If it were difficult at first, I'd just watch men in action, I could smell them a mile away. Their routines were like vaudeville acts at an underground nightclub, like men who still wear love beads and say, "Yeah man." And as for those who think I secretly hate myself and can't look into a mirror, they're the ones who don't get much, who think the bedroom's for sleeping. To tell you the truth, if it weren't for the boredom, for the nonsense I have to put up with to get what I want, I'd have thought I were born into paradise, the place where everyone sits around without clothes, touching themselves, waiting for something to happen, hoping it won't.

The Romance of the Retreat

I remember the night I fell in love with the evening. I was driving on a mountain road, a few moments after dusk: the trees' shadows were merging with the background of the sky, the cool air was a whisper in my ear. I did not abandon myself uncontrollably, I did not lose sight of the road. Rather the evening surrounded me the way a footprint surrounds a foot, the way a star is surrounded by empty space. I lost the notion of preference: I did not care for darkness over light, I could not tell my left hand from my right. Later I drove through the forest knocking down small trees; rabbits were frozen in my headlights, the car's engine gave off the smell of fear: fear released, fear repulsed, fear returning. I got out of the car in a small clearing and turned off the lights. The evening made no demands; I did not have to remove my clothes, there were no promises made or broken. I did not have to give up my other lovers, nor did the idea of fidelity even occur to me: no matter how many times I left the evening it would always come back to me, by choice or otherwise.

The Romance of the Radish

This is what I learned from the art of gardening: the aphid leaves nothing to the leaves, the mole loves to possess by the roots, what you take from the earth you cannot get back. I met a man in the garden once, he said he was without profession. Yet he was always giving advice: plant onions by the cabbage, don't sow the seeds too deep in the ground. In time he invited himself into my house, planted his feet next to mine, shoveled his tongue between my lips. At first I tried to ignore him, I asked him to leave. But something was growing between us: on days he did not come I became impatient with myself, I tore the marigolds up with the weeds. Insects were eating tomatoes from the inside, I did not know how to save them. It turned out I needed his advice.

It was months before he asked me for money, still later before he moved into my bed. Making love, he had the tongue of a chameleon, and afterward the voice of a cricket. He had an aversion to the personal: when I asked him how long he would stay, he said, "I will not leave you. I am a perennial, if I leave I'll come back — like the wild asparagus, I'll pop up where you least expect." I don't know how many times I threatened to leave him, but leaving him would mean leaving my own house, everything I owned.

He never thought me attractive: he loved to tell me how pale I looked, how I did not eat the proper foods. He'd laugh and say no one else would have me. In the winter, he would not see me at all. And in the spring, when the squash and spinach began to sprout, he wrote me letters from someplace distant, told me to water every day and dust the tomatoes, make sure the men in my life would take care of me and get plenty of sun. But when the garden began to bear its full weight, I felt too weak to weed myself, I let the broccoli go to flower, I let everything else go to waste.

The Romance of the Regiment

The general was always giving orders: clean up this mess, have your hair done this way, let me enter from the rear. He had an intense dislike for insects, clumps of dirt, anything small. His hatred of long hair extended only to men; he wanted his women to have hair that would run all the way down their backs, the way a river would divide a battlefield. He'd spend whole nights stroking my hair and whistling military tunes, even if the only thoughts that crossed his mind were the next day's maneuvers, which medals he should pin on his chest. He was reluctant to perform his marital duty, with his wife, with me, or with anyone else.

He went to sleep with his boots off, perfectly erect, his hands at his sides, his feet pointing upward toward heaven like a dead man. He did not love war, and he never struck me in the face, in moments of passion or otherwise. He would do anything for his men short of an act of mercy.

With the general I always ate the best of food, wore gorgeous clothes and rode in limousines. We took short trips to Venezuela to meet the oil magnates, and all his friends called me his paramour. He forbade me to use vulgar language and always made me wear a dress. In public he was attentive and mildly affectionate: always a kiss on the back of the neck, his arm entwined with mine. Sadly, it was all a camouflage; to be perfectly frank, the general was stiff when he should have been soft and vice versa.

The Romance of the Real World

I decided to give up on the world of metaphor: I would become the rose itself. The world would not exceed its own dimensions, nothing would be more or less than it seemed. The streets were deserted and no one would speak to me; luncheonettes were left with their doors open, their half-empty saucers and plates. It was always cloudy out and the cold gray air hung over the city like a cloud of smoke, a drawn-up net. If someone struck a match, the hiss would be heard for miles. If a dress were unzipped, it could set a child on edge.

At first I took everything at face value: I believed the promises of politicians, the husband who happened to come home late. I forgot the nuances between women, the open window of the penthouse looking over the river. I could see everything but I could not touch. If I were prepared to register a feeling, it was without approximation. When a drop of rain reached up from my roots it was like . . . when the sun went down the air was somewhat different: scientists like to call it photosynthesis, but what is that like? And if I speculated on my own death, the moment of my wilting, I would be like the mute actor whose words had failed him once again.

Yes, my frustrations were too numerous to mention: in someone's lapel I smelled pastries rising from the bakery, how would I communicate that? Growing wild in the country, listening to the varieties of weather, there were endless trails of animals who stood above me, who blocked my view. Always my petals seemed like an enormous ear: I could not help but hear what was going on around me. There were teen-agers on a small park bench, acting out a movie they must have seen: "Is it too soon to tell our parents?" "You'll never leave me, will you?" "My intentions are the best." Out of boredom I had to hum myself a tune: an aria of Handel's, a ballad about the agitation of water, the changing seasons, the soft powder of snow.

O the flat world could hold nothing of me, it was like water without the glass. I knew I had to return to the world of metaphor, my own domain: to the flower's fragrant desires, the dangerous thorns of the stem, the petal's opening lips. And I would lose my passion for daily life, its vague and helpless watering, its withered speech and slowly spreading weeds. I would save my kiss for the pollination of the dream life, the windless orchard, the landscape which would not end.

The Romance of the Remainder

At last I've fallen in love with endings. I've begun to dream of being the last woman on earth — by some miracle, disaster or divine plan, only men have survived the holocaust. To satisfy themselves, they had to seek me out. At first I found it thrilling, I slept with anyone, the youngest first and then the strongest. But suddenly I had more power than I was accustomed to, I had too much to choose from! To keep my composure I had to get away from myself. If I sat in a chair a man's hand would be underneath it. If I decided to take a shower a man would be peering from behind the curtain. I covered myself the best I could, I never took favors from anyone; I opened doors for myself, I lifted heavy objects from room to room.

The world was not a desert as you might expect; far from it. When the smoke cleared the foliage was lush, there were weeds growing out of the concrete. I found a million ways to enjoy myself. Empty staircases spoke to me alone; I communed with the empty cars, or the women slumped over the steering wheels. I walked into movie houses and empty screens became my mirrors. My temperament shortly became less extreme, I never wept or raised my voice: I was like the surveyor's plomb in the middle of a valley. When it snowed over the dead bodies and piles of rubble, it was as though the old world had been erased, smeared off-white or slightly gray. And if the end of the world were near, then something else I did not yet understand would soon begin.

In the distance I hear someone playing music on a comb. Two tin cans and a drum. Someone small is lying down with someone else. Like it or not, as though we had a choice, we'll love to survive, we'll refuse anything that refuses to move.